T0069047

START

START

Jean Gallagher

Oberlin College Press
Oberlin, Ohio

Thanks to the journals in which these poems first appeared: *Barrow Street*: "Eleusinian Fauna: Which Animal Is That"; *The Common Review*: "Theogony"; *FIELD*: "Year in Eleusis"; *The Journal*: "Script on Gold Leaf" (1), (3), (6), (8); *Seven Carmine*: "Bitter Green Song"; and to this book's first readers: Sharona Berken, Rosemary Deen, Marie Ponsot, and Bethany Saltman.

The FIELD Poetry Series, vol. 27
Oberlin College Press, 50 N. Professor Street, Oberlin, OH 44074
www.oberlin.edu/ocpress

Cover and book design: Steve Farkas
Cover art: Marilyn Palmeri and Daniel Ricuitto,
Chilly Beginning (detail), 2007. Mixed media on paper.
Photograph: Graham S. Haber, 2011.

Library of Congress Cataloging-in-Publication Data

Gallagher, Jean, 1962-
  Start / Jean Gallagher.
     p. cm. -- (The Field poetry series; vol. 27)
  Includes bibliographical references.
  ISBN 978-0-932440-43-3 (pbk. : alk. paper) -- ISBN 0-932440-43-6 (pbk. : alk. paper)
  I. Title.
  PS3607.A415435S73 2012
  811'.6--dc23
                                        2011048676

For Maggie
and
for David

Contents

One buries children, one gains new children, one dies oneself; and this men take heavily, carrying earth to earth. But it is necessary to harvest life like a fruit-bearing grain, and that one be, the other not.

—Euripides, fragment from the lost play *Hypsipyle*

Theogony

They just keep on
getting born   flung like new
              seconds out
                            of the clock   like brand-
              new elements
just out of the
                    sun's furnace.
                                    Let's get it
              on! the sun keeps
                            shouting and
              they do. All the things
              we'll never get done
                                    are born and
                    born   confetti
              at the wedding   fistfuls and
    fistfuls   the litter
              of petals   the little
                    divine ideas at our feet.

§

Year in Eleusis

Demeter Invents

Not even

        the black shine

in the trees

    heard you

slide

        away

blood

    locket.

Up in the scorchlight

        I invented

the audible

    for you   :

nursery rhyme

        alphabet song

counting game

    hide-and-seek

riddle

        where

did you

    go.

Eleusinian Fauna: Which Animal Is That

The animal in me now mother of nothing
cries like a magdalene told
don't touch
who later hears the new translation
don't hold on.

Eleusinian for Beginners

Stranded is not the word I'd use.

More like: *with without*. What

kind of place?

No, no: not *what kind*, but *how.*

Demeter Settles

Everything I own fits in a suitcase
the size of *meanwhile*, stuffed
with light I can't use.
At first I unpacked nothing
but a new idea
I held in the fire as long as I could.
Little sword, I said, *better get*
tempered. But there were interruptions,
fatal, beautiful
all the same. They told me,

> Live in the *almost*, this Eleusis.
> You can.

Another View of the Origin of the Mysteries at Eleusis

It was the best I could do   something never

enough on fire   something

thrown down and loved.

Reasons to Build the Temple in Eleusis

Somewhere to put the *didn't*
quite   someplace to keep
the boats I use running
the chain of sorrowpools.

Little Famines

Those seeds stay
shut

                          I lost   *where*

                                             did   *how*

               can   *she is*

                              without

The subtracted
pulled under
add up.
How far
can you dig
to find the live one now.

Initiand's Song

Show me why it's all right,
the *is-then-isn't*.
Bring it
into the visible's little
circle of yellow light.

What I lost is ringing
like a telephone somewhere else,
so tell me
what's in the shut basket
in the middle of my life.

Demeter, Mid-Winter

I almost forget what I was
waiting for   leaning up
against the marble house *just
this.*

There's water running
somewhere   how is it
unfrozen   what does it
sound like   *your construction
                project's suspended.
                Take off that hard
                hat and be made.*

Winter Practice

Winter is its own
green season   mind's green
wood not burning   good
for waiting.

How do I do it?
Keep blowing the candle out.

Demeter's Bitter Green Song

A narrow road of bitter green your marrow.
A racecourse of bitter green your sorrow.
A skimcoat of bitter green your striving.
A slipknot of bitter green your love.

Watch for the sun's stoplight to turn bitter green and then run.
Switch your heart's bitter green current back to On.
Ride your eyesight's bitter green tilt-a-whirl till curfew.
Taste this spring's bitter green sugar and say *thank you*.

Demeter Reconsiders

You fell

        through the earth's flowering trapdoor,

        and I learned to love winter's privacies, the being

        nowhere to be seen.

But is that you now,

                rattling the cage in the orphanage

                that underlies everything,

you saying, *I'm back, I'm back,*

                    with your bare foot on the

                    first rung

                    of spring's hard green ladder;

is that spring's green fist in my chest.

Hadean Flora: Demeter Speculates

The light there   maybe

houses lilacs   species

labeled *What-You-Don't-Know*.

She might come carrying some.

What Else She Might Come Carrying

Her own shut basket
which stone gifts
whose voice calling her
what first name.

Demeter Dreams

The dream plummets into
the black water I never knew
was passable   I thought
was black rock

So what was it like
the time away
with nothing but
world to catch you

You say

I ate

every

day's

red seed

You say

I ate

I grew

Start

Incipit   She's starting   not

                      somehow   without me

semper   cut from the same

                      bolt of green as all

vita   my lost ones   the same

                      ever   walking soon

nova   her footsteps   and theirs

                      and mine   green starts.

How Not

She'll be back not
as I thought but
as spring's mind does.

New Map of Eleusis

The sky's glass

lock cracks   earth's black leather door

swings wide

Can you see now

how each life leads in two directions   away

and away

§

Hymns for Birthmothers: Aphrodite

I couldn't help myself sleeping

with what I knew would go

kablooey. I thought n

was constant but now my mind off

its leash is crowded with the calculus for

what undoes next. The name I chose

for it means *unerasable*

mark where I touched

down but that will change.

I just won't know

to what. My name

will be new then

too   turned to nothing but *not*.

Hymns for Birthmothers: Maia

At school I studied sorrow's spiral
notebook down to the last line
and I practiced the scales every day.
But there's a new music now
that tells you how things came to be and how
they are arranged and something
was killed to make it. Nothing has ever mattered

more to me than this.

Hymns for Birthmothers: Leto

I went from rock to rock but each said *not*

here. I finally sat on some stone

steps leading up to nothing

but a little market where *found*

and *needed* and *lost* were the

one apple. *Please take what*

I have to give you I said and that's when

I knew what I wanted

to put down was the arrow in me always

pointing somewhere else.

Hymns for Birthmothers: Dryope

I ran because I was

afraid   what I had

made was so

complete   so without

me. I know luck

wrapped it in its hijacked

fur. I know this

was the equivalent of everything.

Hymns for Birthmothers: Metis

I thought I'd go the whole

way but got swallowed

by the state of things.

Something else embodies me now,

something I used to love.

Hymns for Birthmothers: Semele

I wanted for a change to see
what was true and the world
said *if you insist.* I knew it
might burn but not how much or
how fast. I didn't have the chance to
say *world, keep this one unfinished*
thing safe a little longer. Sew this into
yourself. But the world did anyway.

§

Telesterion Sound Check (1)

*In all-night dances and in the darkness of the Telesterion (the
Hall of Initiation), the mystery initiates moved out of time and
the parameters by which they normally defined their world.*

Is it the baby

waking at night

is it the body saying

something   something

Telesterion Sound Check (2)

It's like the air itself
knows your name. Except it's not
a name you've ever heard before.

Telesterion Sound Check (3)

What you're hearing is not so much
the heart as its holes. World running
in, murmuring. Running out.

Telesterion Sound Check (4)

That undermusic   the body's
hum   we hold
all the hades in our mouths
and do not open them.

Telesterion Sound Check (5)

Listen how the nightfloor offers

its tracks to light's needle

how we ride our red wagons

to ruin in that music   *there's a life*

you don't know

and it's this one.

The Lesser Mysteries (1)

Even if you've killed something
you love there is a way
in. You can still be taken
apart by hunger. You can
still have your pieces
put in a stone box and shaken.
You can still be put back
together to feel the scorch of things coming
to be as they are.

The Lesser Mysteries (2)

You have to start and then start. Here. No.
Here. Carried   taken   whatever
you call it   going somewhere leaning
like love against the stitching   the until.

The Greater Mysteries (1)

Carved out in me as god used

to be. Bruised into

me where a new tree

spikes. Gold pitch

sticks to what broke where now

green reaches. This love is where nobody is

standing, where I did.

I, crescent. In which direction. We call

the moon *crescent* either way.

The Greater Mysteries (2)

I came out of the mystery hall
feeling like a stranger to myself.

squinting out

into the sunlight   every rock

I'm made of crowbarred

up and moved. And still moving. The hard

hats   the picks and shovels   the shouts   *eleusis*

arrival   is ongoing.

§

Script on Gold Leaf (1)

*(Either Fate overcame me
or the star-flinger with lightning.)*

Grief's thunderpunch took me down

where the light's like the back of a dropped gold shovel.

I ate grief's thick gold toast!

I drank grief's big gold soup!

Grief's jewelry, look out for it, heavy on my wrist!

Look at this gold duffelbagful!

Tell me how to take it off.

Show me where to put it down.

No? Not yet? OK, then, show me

how to root my feet in this gold

field and be the thing that grows.

Script on Gold Leaf (2)

(The mindful one seizes Kore)

The gold name of what you
    wanted: Fallen-Through.
The gold fishnet whistles two
    tunes at once: *catch-release.*

Script on Gold Leaf (3)

*(There is a spring at the right side,
and standing by it a white cypress.
Thirst [untranslatable].)*

Even now, after the shine

on my ideas shook off in tinsel, I still

want things. Thirst is a handful

of local grit you can pick up glittering

anywhere. Thirst is a native tree

all over. When I got to the water,

they said *and you are . . . ?* I said *I've been*

leaning against this white-hot cypress,

reaching, all my life.

Script on Gold Leaf (4)

(You, tell them the whole entire truth.
Say: I am a child of Earth and Starry Sky.
My name is "Starry.")

Where I'm from *a little far light* and *the dirt*

    right under my feet are the same word.

My name means *like light but not*

    exactly.

My name means *visible now because of how dark*

    things have gotten.

My name means *you can see me but only as*

    I was.

Script on Gold Leaf (5)

*(Ahead you will find from the Lake of Memory
cold water pouring forth.)*

Forget it is the silver slick where everything

you did skidded.

Can you remember is the gold roadbed

you can't see bearing

what leaves and leaves.

      And the lake? Drive your life straight

in   *surface* just another

name for what's next

to what's next.

Script on Gold Leaf (6)

*(They will ask you
by what necessity you have come.)*

Take the gold pill to stay awake.

Keep the gold bit in your teeth until

you can tell them about your skidmark life, how

the skidmark washed away.

Script on Gold Leaf (7)

(I have paid the penalty.
I have flown out of the heavy, difficult circle.)

Sure I paid for leaning on the scale   paid

everything.   Pocketbook emptied   I spun away

not from the griefs but from their goldweight   riding

my life   a round tin sled   down [?]   cold [?]

maybe   but at this speed   can you believe it

a gladness to be had in suffering what you never

suffered before.   Kid   kid   light and clumsy

with *never*   with *not*   I kept falling and am never not.

Script on Gold Leaf (8)

(They will ask you what you are seeking.)

Roll down the gold hill. You'll
be met and met. Everything will
crowd to ask

> *what are you*

> > something moving fast

> *looking for*

> > where I am not

> *what else have*
> *you ever been*

§

Persephone (1)

I pulled up the beautiful
      thing I wanted
and the ground I never knew
      could open did. The ground is not
a solid. It is honey-
      combed with room and whatever
way there is
      is exactly
what gives way.

Persephone (2)

What I'm falling
through is the cloth
of things   the one I'm
cut from. Is it really that
far below me   what never stops.

Persephone (3)

I didn't know until I
fell away that I am what keeps
happening   a breaking-
into. Even my clay
heart knows it now and
flowers   howling.

Persephone (4)

The girl I lost through
the hole in me was me.
I said *what happened to*
my life and that was winter.
My life came back from marrying
knowing something really red.

And spring is asking *can I learn   am I*
learning   yes I am   to love this
husband enough.

Theory of Pomegranate Seed (1)

What keeps *elsewhere*
alive in me.
There's always   isn't there
a hole in the world.

Persephone (5)

I thought I was single and then landed
in everything-included   even the
could-have-but-didn't   even the *did-and-*
then-was-sorry. At first I didn't
want them   the little bright
leadweights I was made
to eat. But long
marriage   tree in the black
basement of things   you are
not what I thought. Far
greener. Reaching down
much farther in the dark.

Theory of Pomegranate Seed (2)

Bloody delicious with its inedible
heart: *this will change.*

Persephone (6)

Birdfall   leafdrift   whatever drops
through here leaves
a black line but just in the mind.

Persephone (7)

What feels like
falling   a green always
opening. Anyone can
say it   I am a way.

§

Works and Days

(February 27, 2008)

Few call this day by its true name.

Today is the day to open
        the jar of what-next.
Today is the day the big animals
        in you start pulling.
Today is the day your boat touches
        water and knows that home
is motion. Somebody else
        knows today's first
name but we can still call it
        found. We can call it
whatever we do.

Notes

Demeter Settles: According to the Homeric *Hymn to Demeter*, after her daughter Persephone is abducted by Hades, Demeter goes to the Greek city of Eleusis, where she disguises herself and becomes the nursemaid to the son of the ruling household. She decides she will make the child immortal by burying him in the hearth-fire every night, while the household sleeps. However, the child's mother, Metaneira, wakes one night and, not understanding Demeter's intentions, cries aloud and interrupts the process.

Another View of the Origins of the Mysteries at Eleusis and **Reasons to Build the Temple At Eleusis**: After Metaneira interrupts Demeter's efforts to immortalize her child, Demeter casts the child to the ground; his sisters pick him up and attempt to comfort him. Demeter reveals herself and asks that the citizens of Eleusis build a temple for her where she will teach them her Mysteries, religious rites that offer initiates a happier existence on earth and in the afterlife.

Initiand's Song: One aspect of Demeter's Mysteries involved the carrying of a closed basket containing ritual objects.

Telesterion Sound Check (1): Epigraph is from Helene P. Foley, ed., *The Homeric* Hymn to Demeter (Princeton University Press, 1993).

The Greater Mysteries (2): Epigraph is from Sopatros, *Rhetores Graeci*, quoted in Foley. The Greek noun *eleusis* means "arrival."

Scripts on Gold Leaf: The original scripts on gold leaf are a set of gold tablets, used by members of a cult devoted to Persephone and Dionysus, found in gravesites in Southern Italy and Greece, the oldest dating to around 400 BCE. The tablets were often placed in the mouths of the dead; most contained instructions for negotiating the passage into the underworld, including instructions for how to address Persephone and other chthonic guardians. Epigraphs with excerpts from the tablets are adapted from translations found in *Ritual Texts for the Afterlife*, by Fritz Graf and Sarah Iles Johnston (Routledge, 2007).

Works and Days: Epigraph is from Hesiod, *Works and Days*, translated by R. M. Frazer (University of Oklahoma Press, 1983).